MAKE IT MOVE

MARLA CONN

A Division of
Carson Dellosa Education

Photo Glossary

 cart

 pull

 push

 rope

 sled

 swing

 **wagon**

 **weeds**

I can make it move.

cart

I push the **cart.**

5

I can make it move.

wagon

I pull the **wagon.**

I can make it move.

sled

I push the **sled.**

I can make it move.

weeds

I pull the **weeds.**

I can make it move.

swing

I push the **swing.**

I can make it move.

rope

I pull the **rope.**

Activity

1. In small groups, discuss how you can make things move.

2. On a separate sheet of paper, draw a picture of pulling and pushing.

I can move something by pushing.	I can move something by pulling.

3. What is happening in each picture? Talk about it.